MORTAL MISTAKES

by Charis Mather

Minneapolis, Minnesota

Credits

All images are courtesy of Shutterstock.com, unless otherwise specified. With thanks to Getty Images, Thinkstock Photo, and iStockphoto. Background texture throughout – Abstracto. Front Cover – Trialsanderrors. 4&5 – urfin, MR.Yanukit, studiovin, Anneka. 6&7 – Daxiao Productions, Everett Collection, xpixel, M. Schuppich, Maitree Rimthong. 8&9 – Cait Thompson, Valentin Agapov, Lia Koltyrina, buengza. 10&11 – Viliam.M, Hoika Mikhail, Brandon Bourdages. 12&13 – Stephen Barnes, Vasin Lee, luanateutzi. 14&15 – MF production, V.Leers, Le Petit Parisien. 16&17 – Elenamiv, hdy1guy, Agence de presse Meurisse. 18&19 – Jules Porreau, Danussa. 20&21 – Dana.S, Imagentle, Luigi Rados, Trialsanderrors. 22&23 – wavebreakmedia, EloPaint, rozbyshaka, Andrawaag.

Bearport Publishing Company Product Development Team

President: Jen Jenson; Director of Product Development: Spencer Brinker; Managing Editor: Allison Juda; Associate Editor: Naomi Reich; Senior Designer: Colin O'Dea; Associate Designer: Elena Klinkner; Associate Designer: Kayla Eggert; Product Development Specialist: Anita Stasson

Library of Congress Cataloging-in-Publication Data is available at www.loc.gov or upon request from the publisher.

ISBN: 979-8-88822-005-4 (hardcover)
ISBN: 979-8-88822-190-7 (paperback)
ISBN: 979-8-88822-320-8 (ebook)

© 2024 Booklife Publishing
This edition is published by arrangement with Booklife Publishing.

North American adaptations © 2024 Bearport Publishing Company. All rights reserved. No part of this publication may be reproduced in whole or in part, stored in any retrieval system, or transmitted in any form or by any means, electronic, mechanical, photocopying, recording, or otherwise, without written permission from the publisher.

For more information, write to Bearport Publishing, 5357 Penn Avenue South, Minneapolis, MN 55419.

CONTENTS

Strange Lives, Stranger Deaths. . 4
Bobby Leach 6
Draco of Athens. 10
Franz Reichelt 14
Sophie Blanchard 18
Nasty Ways to Go 22
Glossary 24
Index 24

STRANGE LIVES, STRANGER DEATHS

The past is full of stories about people who lived in strange ways. Many died in strange ways, too.

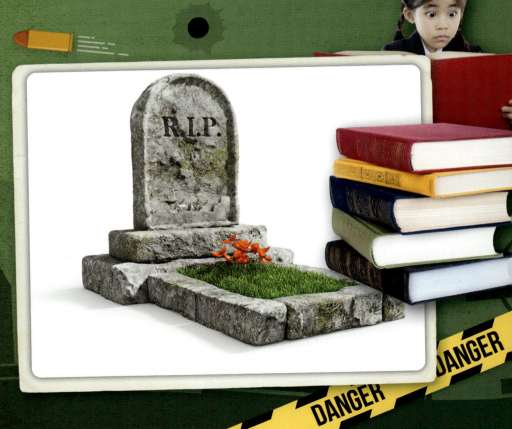

It takes only one **mortal** mistake to meet an awful end. Some people found that out the hard way.

BOBBY LEACH

HIS MISTAKE: AN ORANGE PEEL

Bobby Leach did many **dangerous** tricks. People always thought one of these tricks would kill him.

Bobby once went over Niagara Falls!

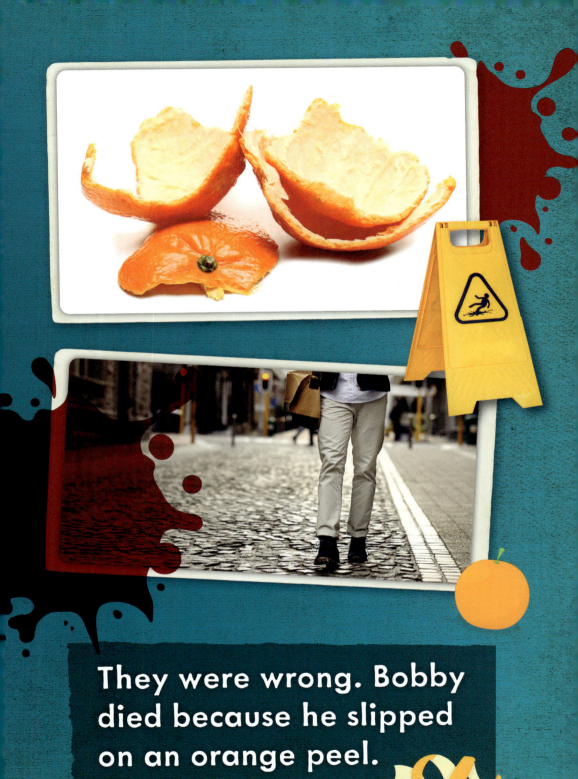

They were wrong. Bobby died because he slipped on an orange peel.

Bobby hurt his leg badly when he fell. Doctors cut it off to stop him from getting sick.

But this did not help. Bobby got sicker and died.

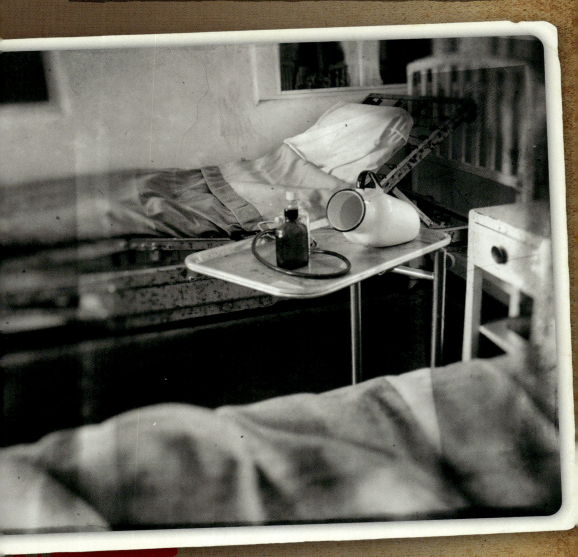

Who knew fruit could be so dangerous?

9

DRACO OF ATHENS

HIS MISTAKE: POPULARITY

Draco of Athens was known for making many laws.

They were some of the first laws written down.

Many of his laws were **strict.** They made life hard for people.

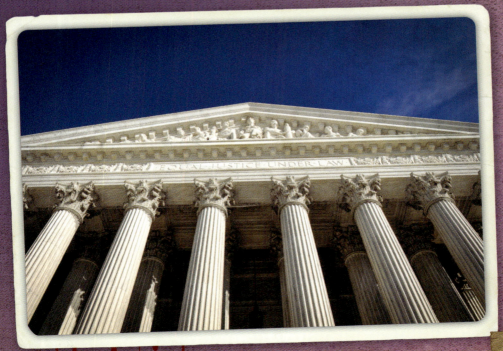

However, many people still liked Draco. One day, they saw him at a show.

At the time, people used to throw clothes at people they liked.

People threw clothes at Draco. Soon, he was buried under them and died.

Too bad there were no laws about throwing clothes!

FRANZ REICHELT

HIS MISTAKE: A COAT

Franz Reichelt was a tailor. His job was to make clothes.

But Franz wanted to do more.

He wanted to fly. Franz made a coat to help him fall slowly, just as a **parachute** would.

The tailor first tested his coat using **dummies**. They landed safely . . . sometimes. Franz decided to try it himself.

Franz climbed up the Eiffel Tower. He jumped. But his coat did not work. Franz died.

The Eiffel Tower

Kersplat!

SOPHIE BLANCHARD

HER MISTAKE: FIREWORKS

Hot-air balloons were a big part of Sophie Blanchard's life. They would also be part of her death.

People used to pay to see Sophie flying her balloon. She was the first woman with this job.

One time, Sophie set off **fireworks** while flying. Her balloon was set on fire.

Sophie and her burning balloon fell from the sky. That was the end of poor Sophie.

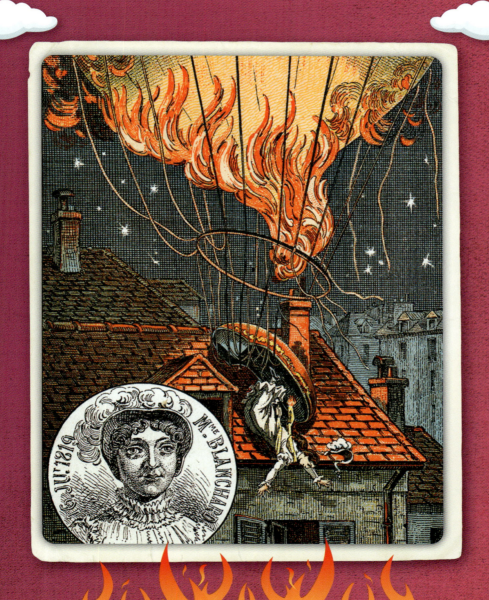

NASTY WAYS TO GO

Bobby, Draco, Franz, and Sophie found out their mistakes the hard way. Who do you think made the worst mistake?

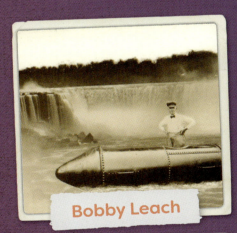
Bobby Leach

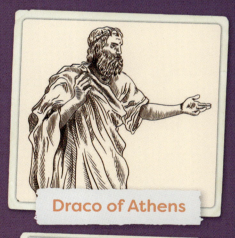
Draco of Athens

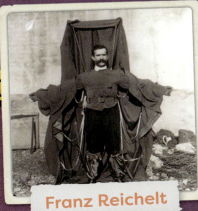
Franz Reichelt

Sophie Blanchard

These people met their ends from an orange peel, too many clothes, a coat, and fireworks.

Which was the nastiest way to go?

GLOSSARY

dangerous not safe

dummies human-shaped objects used for tests

fireworks things that make lots of colorful sparks when set on fire

hot-air balloons large fabric balloons that can lift people into the sky

mortal causing or having caused death

parachute a soft cloth attached to ropes that is used to slow a fall

strict extreme and harsh

INDEX

balloons 18–21
clothes 12–14, 23
coat 14–17, 23
Eiffel Tower 17
fire 20

fireworks 18, 20, 23
leg 8
parachutes 15
peel 6–7, 23
tricks 6